MY GOD IS NO MAN

POEMS

SARAH OROPEZA

MY GOD IS NO MAN

SARAH OROPEZA

ISBN: 979-8-218-08602-2

Editor: Ethan Kumke & Alexis Briones
Cover and internal design © 2022 Sarah Oropeza

First printing edition, 2022

Sarah Oropeza
www.ohsarahlee.com
@ohsarahlee_

For all the times I did not choose myself

CONTENTS:

III

IV

I

To us it was love, just not the kind that leaves you filled

TERRIBLE

Tell me the truth
about who you are.
I will show you, it's ok.
I have been terrible too.

IT BURNS WHEN YOU TOUCH IT
after Alysia Nicole Harris @poppyinthewheat

I came out of my mother, someone's premeditated wife. Breasts filled with innocent milk long before lactation. Hips destined for childbearing. Named after my father, who's named after a man who abandoned him, then came back just in time to see all his granddaughters are too branded with his last name. He says, "At least through one of them, I'll make it into heaven."

I imagine God flipping a coin and chuckling at the outcome of the sex. Another girl. Another mother. Another vacant uterus. Another unclaimed body. Another continent. Another well for men to rinse off their last names.

When my daughter left my hips, my blood ruled over the white linen beneath me like a river of ancestral women desperate for a way out. As if it were a warning that this wasn't the worst part of the story.

Is that what you meant, Lord? That childbirth hurts, but the real pain bleeds through when he leaves you to raise her alone. Which last name do I place my daughter in? Mine or his? Both names are drowning with men who leave. Both fathered by imagery and mothers. Both are looking for an heir that doesn't run from home.

During the early hours of motherhood, I doubted that my young spine could carry what was expected. No Abraham for this Sarah. No 90-year wait. I cradled my fatherless child against my dedicated chest, unable to find a bible verse that would keep us. Does this mean I'm off the hook? Does this mean single mothers get a do-over? Does this mean you will still punish me?

When the men find me, they can smell the burning bible pages I ignite to keep my daughter warm. They do not question why I reek of ash, they only question why I don't crumble at the sight of their brow. They only question why it burns to touch me. This well has been dried for some time. There is no water left. There is no woman here to rename.

Lord, if my anatomy has been staged, maybe it's because you knew I would never kneel before you otherwise. You should've known; I'd take my grandfather's last name from him and make a mantra out of it, turn it into an heirloom my family is proud of, turn it into a woman-owned business, into something better, like a book.

Is it a crime, Lord, to tell them my saving isn't in a man but in the poem of my daughter's face? Is it a crime, Lord, to tell them my God doesn't leave her children when life swallows her? My God does not ask women to submit in a home they built with their bare hands. My God does not reek of men who cannot pick up a mother's-tired feet.

Is it a crime, Lord, to tell them, my God is no man?

After the alarm went off the fourth time, he'd finally climb out of bed. His footsteps sounded like mini earthquakes hitting the faded, outdated carpet. Sighs escaped from his body while he brushed his teeth. They would travel up the stairs like they were running from more than just his internal prison. I didn't know what he was so heavy with then. At some point, I stopped trying to figure out how many empty days full of longing were weighing him down. I used to imagine they were dreams of who he wanted to be before he had all these kids, where he'd go, who he'd morph into, or who he'd love if it was Mom or some other woman that could handle his shit.

I could hear the engine of his company truck through the thinning walls. The ripe tires glided over the gravel in the driveway. I used to close my eyes and pretend I was the gravel, covered in the ocean's brine, swallowed in a life that doesn't mimic an ignored pain. "Get up! We are going to be late!" Mom would shout. She took on each morning like a chore that never ended. And Mom never cried in front of us. So when she did, it was like an unexpected storm that shook you out of deep sleep. She carried something without a proper name; no new car could take its place. It was more than a runaway dream. Many days I tried to muster up the courage to tell her, "I feel it too." But I was only thirteen, kept getting into fights, and challenged every quote in the bible.

"Girl, I said get up!" mom would shout from the kitchen. The mini vacation in my head would have to wait till tomorrow. I'd cover my skin in the hand-me-down catholic school uniform that hated me. It couldn't cover up the truth in me; it couldn't eucharist my body into a holy one that doesn't question men or their god. It could taste the sin on my skin; it could taste me.

All five of us kids would climb into the van dad bought mom to help with the sadness. We didn't have any money, so dad worked seven days a week. While mom did what moms do - everything else. All we knew about life then was that mom played Martina McBride's "A Broken Wing" every morning in the car. All we knew was that dad always worked to pay off our school and that van and those hospital bills reeking of miscarriages Mom had before Pablo was born. All we knew was that mom got us to school, no matter how sad she was. And that we all hate this schedule of life, the way one hates church on Sunday when you want to rest from barely surviving the week. All we knew was that tomorrow was inching its way toward us like a ritual and that we would go another day without the courage to look at life in the face and say, "I'm done!"

I'M NOT FROM HERE

I don't belong to a country.
No land wants me kept,
no language I call my own.
My body is a border.
I am somewhere between two places
same time zones with different faces.
When they ask me where I'm from,
I tell them,
"I come from all the wounds we forget to tend to."
My people are the poets who bleed
through truth and scratch paper.
We have the same gaping tongue,
searching for a place that looks like us.
Only to find different faces with different hair.
Only to find our homelands are stuck inside
the void of a wound.

CHURCH

He lays me on my back like roses on an altar.
Reads the sacred scripture on my skin.
Uses his tongue, then his hands.
He brings the sin. I take the confession.
Except there is nothing in between us.
Our faces exposed like the truth.
He lets it all out.
His heart weeps like heavy rainfall.
He only comes here to repent.
To pour out each pain rooted in him all over my body.
He shoves his hips between my sore thighs.
I moan a prayer in his ear.
He takes the communion of me with his teeth.
Amen," he says.
He holds me on his chest.
I can hear his heart beating fast.
We do not sing psalms when we finish.
He is full.
I am the spoken word he needed for the week.
He leaves.
"He will come back," I tell myself.
I wait until he remembers that I am as forgiving,
and as loving, as a god on Sundays.

WHERE I COME FROM

I come from my mother's old pain,
from my father's generational anger.
My first name, a ticking time bomb.
My last name, gunsmoke.
I taste like war, my skin, a battlefield.
Can you hear the women in me crying?
Can you see the men in me bleeding?
My ancestors have made a safe zone out of me.
Who is coming to help me when the blue sky turns gray?
Who will help me when hope begins to narrow by the second?
Is it you?
Can you promise to wipe my tears,
to run your hands through my hair?
Can you cover up my body with more than
just your imagery of what I look like naked?
Can I make your mouth a shelter to hide in, to belong to,
when I've run out of words to convince the generations housed in
me that the pain ends here, in this book?
What if I don't get it all out?
What happens if I can't pour another book out of my hands?
Can you carry the empty spaces of me?
Until I can fill them back up with poems?
You can chase me down with whiskey
and other women.
Just help me numb the pain.
Help me forget that war lives here.
Help me forget where I come from.

UNHIDABLE
after Elizabeth Acevedo @acevedowrites

I give myself a pep talk at every door.
"Look people in the eyes, so they don't notice."
"Speak loudly so they are too intimidated to approach you."
I turn myself into a machine gun,
asking questions only I know the answers to.
Making men feel small with intellectual statements
that take away from my body;
to cover me up, to get their eyes off me.
I cannot hide myself any more than I already do.
My earthquake voice doesn't always scare them.
Sometimes it brings attention to my lips, another curve;
another thing men want to take. Another reason to banish
lipgloss from my purse. To cover-up. To disappear.
Another reason to vacate from a body that I didn't ask for.

NO FUNERAL

I am sixteen.
My womb is a deflated balloon.
The god I just gave birth to
has a head full of silk hair.
The boy I cannot breathe without
doesn't know his daughter is the promised land.

My father sits in the lobby for hours,
convincing himself that he has enough
money to feed us all.
The teenage girl in me dies.

Womanhood sinks into my body.
She molds herself inside my blood,
teaching me how to carry
generations of discomfort.

I homeschool myself
to breastfeed the baby,
enroll myself in college,
graduate with honors,
cry myself to sleep.
The teenage girl in me dies.

I have stretch marks
instead of drunk stories.
I change diapers
instead of changing boyfriends.
My trophies are all the nights
I did not run away from home.

I sleep when the baby sleeps.
I do not know a bed
without sharing it with a smaller body.
I do not know my body without
sharing it with another human.

I do not know my body.
The teenage girl in me dies.

No one ever asks if it hurts,
if it still lingers around my face,
if it still finds me while I dream.

No one ever asks
if the young version of me
is still looking for all the things
she didn't know she had lost.

No one ever asks
if she is still waiting,
if she is still dying.

WHAT THEY DID NOT TEACH YOU

Your curves showed up early.
The men came hunting shortly after.
Making made a fantasy out of you.
Like they didn't have wives at home
with their hands between their legs.

You tried to fight back. Nothing ever worked.
Not baggy clothes or a shotgun for a voice.
Not even the line between your eyebrows,
warning everyone not to fuck with you.

How many times did you hear someone tell you,
"You should smile more. You look so mean,"
instead of asking if you feel safe enough to smile.
You have knives on your tongue, words so sharp
you could slit a throat, and it's not your fault.

Your whole life, you've been protecting yourself
from all the men who left you half-eaten.
From all the men who left you to pick up the pieces.
From all the men who left you and your children
and keep leaving.

Your redwood spine has taken hits so well
people confuse your scars for bragging rights.
Never asking why you never sit down.
Never asking why you don't know how to rest.
They don't see that the patriarchy stole you
and your body by the time your mother birthed you.

They don't see that as a girl, catholic school
and society demanded you submit.
Demanded you cover up your God-given body,
so the grown men don't beg you for a taste

They nick-named you Eve and your pussy Eden,

then had the audacity to call something
so magical original sin.

And I know they tried to hide you.
But I'm here to tell you; you have eyes that cast
spells on their own. Your skin is an alter all by itself.
Anyone who approaches you is an offering.
You were born a goddess.

QUESTIONS FOR MY PARENTS

Who do you want to be?
Who is someone you look up to?
Can you see yourself traveling the world?
Why won't you travel the world?
How many lovers did you have?
Do you still love each other?
Does the pain still linger?
Can you smell out one another
in a room full of strangers?
Do you look at your children
and see each other's faces?
When looking at me, do you ever think
I'm the daughter who doesn't follow the rules?
Do you ever look at me and see God?
Do you know that life isn't over yet,
that there is still time to chase after
the dreams waiting for you?
Do you know that I look at you and think
about all the days you didn't run after
yourselves, and how many days you looked
in our small eyes and could visualize a better life for us?
Do you know that you did it?
You gave us a better life.

FIRST HOME | MOTHERS
after Nayyirah Waheed "Lands"

Sometimes our first home gets burned down,
washed away by pain, ripped apart by distrust.

Some nights I want to go back to my first home.
I want to be held by her, to feel her safe fingertips
making a poem out of my face.

I want to listen to her voice plant itself in my ears,
I want her eyes loving me again.
The eyes she had before she was torn down.

THE KILL

after Thirty Seconds to Mars
for Maria

It would loop for hours on Guitar Hero. As if she was begging someone to notice the hidden poem. Play a game, play the song, over and over until the pain oozes itself out. Like a hangover seeping from your insides after drinking yourself into accepting what you are.

Not the daughter they prayed for, not the daughter they imagined. Instead, a daughter as strong as iron. I know Zeus crawled out of her mouth one night. You can't change my mind.

Her hair used to run down her back like vines before she pruned away the parts that no longer served her. Those long curls sprung like spring. I would use a whole bottle of gel to scrunch my hair to look like hers, just for it to end up looking like dried grass after the first winter freeze. And I didn't care. She was the coolest.

She was Guitar Heroes' best, with two fists dedicated to my call. And like sunrise, they showed up tireless and unbruised. She'd fight right next to me, floating like the music notes on the TV screen. I could hear the music in her stance, "Come Break Me Down!" as she swung to defend me. "I am finished with you!" Her fists telling a deeper story.

The girls that hated me didn't realize I had an older sister who hated something more. Hated she couldn't shout to mom and dad, "THIS IS WHO I REALLY AM!" She was done pretending to be the daughter whose destiny is to marry someone's church-going son.

She just played guitar hero, hoping someone could hear her voice in those lyrics so she didn't have to come out more than she already did. She even dated boys to give the lesbian in her a break from all the fighting in her head.

And then I'd call and only have to say "Sister." And she knew. "Who's fucking with you?" As if the need for her in my voice had

18

a special accent. Like it dressed up in a tone only she could hear clearly. Like the song to the ears of anyone who knows what it's like to have to hide away pieces of yourself to be accepted. Like a prayer to God.

To this day, she answers me on the first ring. Ready for my need of her, ready for the iron she's made out of. Prepared to put a bitch in the ground who doesn't accept me for me. Just ready. Always ready.

For *The Kill*.

SEARCHING

My mother has died many times.
Picked her own flowers,
attended her own funerals.

The worst death for me
was when she left for a while,
and didn't come back the same.
Each one of her deaths
has been set in stone in my pupils,
like a graveyard.

Each time a worse death than before.
Each time a hurt too deep, I drown.

My mother is like the seasons.
I take the summers of her with desperation.
They keep me warm when winter shows up
and she's gone again.

My mother is like a house, except when I visit,
the front door is different.
I don't get to stay long.

Perhaps I will find her in another life
as a field of flowers and I, a bee.
Always finding her the same way as she left.

REMEDY FOR GRIEF

I keep you alive with your picture on the mantle.
Cook your favorite meals, fill my belly, and
declare I had a piece of you.

I plant flowers,
name them all after you,
give them the best soil, and
pretend you're growing back to me.

I knew you'd be gone one day,
just not this fast,
like the way dawn used to sneak up
on us in the morning.

Whenever someone says your name,
the hairs on my body stand up.
As if each has a heartbeat of its own.
Like each one is waiting for your fingertips
to give them attention again.

It hurts to laugh.
It feels like I'm sinning.
Like I'm committing some ruthless crime.
Like I'm doing life without you.
I'm doing life without you.

You are a world away from me.
The only place I can visit you is in my head.
I'm vacationing to death there.

Keeping you alive in small ways
probably disrupts your rest.
I'm sorry.
This is how I stay alive too.

AN ACQUIRED TASTE

I pull out all of mom's books from underneath the bed.
I undress the catholic girl skin, rip off the rosary,
and reveal the real me full of desire to taste sin.

I patiently touch the books like sacred offerings,
with almost naked women and almost naked men
spreading across each cover.

The chapters swollen with loving two men at once,
never having children, being free, and leaving
and leaving and leaving.

They smell like an old secret, like a life unlived,
like a life. Each book - a peek into my mother's head.

I imagine her reading them with eagerness,
digging her nails into the spine, creating a new world
in her head, escaping the small green house she's raising us in.

All those books, unfinished by me, too scared
to be caught with the truth. Too afraid Mom would
find out that I knew there was another way to live.
That I knew sin is an acquired taste.

A FAMILY RESEMBLANCE

He sits across the table,
and I tell myself,
"I do not look like him at all."
I guess heirlooms can be
hidden like that.
Underneath the surface
and stretched out in the hemoglobin.
A family resemblance, not on my face.
But crawling off my violent tongue,
swimming in my lungs, stuck underneath
the withering years without his blank pupils.
And I, like my father,
carry his last name like a second heart.
He doesn't know, all my life,
I've looked for love that maybe,
he was supposed to give me.
His hereditary emptiness
drowns inside of me,
in my words,
in my pen,
in this book.

MY BODY IS THE YARD YOUR WEEDS INVADE

I pull out the weeds stationed in the front yard.
The sun abuses the back of my neck
as sweat finds an exit from my skin.
They told me to keep busy,
make use of these shaken hands.
"It will help with the depression."
For a moment in the heat wave,
I'm washed clean of your torturous memory.
My second mouth - my inner thighs,
forgets about your invasion
and for the first time in a while,
it isn't begging to be sewn shut.
It feels good to rip the weeds out by the scalp.
I'd give anything to expel you
from the pit of my core the same way.
I leave the yard gutted.
Nothing left but dirt and a few earthworms.
Weeds can't grow in a dead yard.
Is my body next?

INITIATION

I hold my legs back like a slingshot,
wait for birth to rip me apart,
with her sharp nails and bloody teeth,
as she demands the woman inside of me to come out.
My young body is forcing itself to fit into
shoes three sizes too big.
The nurse asks, "Are you ready?"
But I don't know how to give birth,
they don't teach you that part.
My mother cradles my face but doesn't speak.
Does she know something that I don't?
The girl empties from of my hips,
bloods stench finds my nostrils,
like instinct, I grow a new pair of feet.
I molt out of the layer of youth,
into a woman, I have never been.

STILL THE ONE

Years have passed,
and seasons have made their appearance.
Hours and hours of moving on to
different cities with different faces.
Changed the furniture around a hundred times.
I even tried falling in love again.
Yet I still think of you first when I write,
as if the words ache to hear a love story,
even if I'm the ending of it.

LESSON

You taught me it is possible to drown,
without being held underwater.

II

Telling the truth is an act of love

QUESTION

Love?
Have you forgiven me yet?
For handing all of you away each time I found
someone new to love and never giving any to myself.

JUST THOUGHTS

1. Half-written poems are aging in my drawers, uncelebrated. I'm not sure if it's because I have writer's block or because all I'm feeling is beginning to go numb from the pressure to write shit down.

2. I came out of my mother homesick, in need to claim something as my own. I watched the women in my family harvest love out of their pain, watched my father work until blood spilled from his voice. All this aching and nowhere to house it, nowhere for it to go home to.

3. When our dog died, I didn't even cry. Death to me was already like an unknown sister you meet at adult age; someone I couldn't relate to but had to love anyway.

4. The first time I fell in love, it wasn't with myself. There are no mirrors that look back at me the way he did.

5. I'm 30 and still get asked when I will find a husband. I still get asked who it is that I'm dating. Like that's the most exciting part about me; who's fucking me. I could say, "Actually, I'm back at church!" And that would be enough. As long as it's a man getting me on my knees. As long as it's a man filling up my throat with his blood and body. As long as it's a fucking man.

6. My parents were not in love. They were at war. I've confused the two my entire life.

7. When you kiss her down her back, does it remind you of all the times I gave you mine to lean on when she wasn't around?

8. I saw my rapist at a bar. I have forgiven him, but he hasn't forgiven himself. I can tell by the way he stays quiet, shrinks into himself when I walk past, shrivels up when my voice makes its way to his neck. Sometimes, I wonder if it was worth it to him. If fucking a half-dead woman whom he couldn't make cum, gave

him the power he so desperately needed. And I know he can't get the image of my face out of his head. Who forgets eyes that can't look back at you? Every time he sees me, he remembers that I'm his living graveyard no one brings flowers to in his honor. Every time he thinks of me, he will always remember he will never be good enough to fuck me while I'm sober.

9. I will fuck you up if you ever fuck with my little sister.

10. Have you found yourself yet, my love, or was I the only one looking for you?

11. I almost killed myself in my basement once, then I heard a voice say, "Mommy, will you play with me?" So, I got up and played Transformers with my son. Transformed myself into a bright-eyed, don't-know-what-a-frown-is woman. Because, when you're a mother, it doesn't matter what's emptying you. The only thing that matters is that you don't run out of things to fill others up with. That your well doesn't run dry. That you don't die in a basement. That you get up. That you get up and make dinner.

12. You still feel me because I still pray for you.

13. I'm still on this come down from you. I still feel you in my bones. Housed like a guest that overstayed its welcome. I'm a prison full of your memory, and I'm afraid to let it go. I'm afraid that when I do, I'll forget your face. I'll forget the way you loved me. I'll forget how to love again. I'll forget what it's like to be ached for, to be needed, to be called "Home."

14. I'm a first-generation college graduate. I have a psychology degree from The University of Kansas. So yes, I psychoanalyze every person I date. Find where their mothers couldn't love them, reveal it was their father's fault. Even then, they still can't love me better. And I'm so sick of it. And I'm so sick of society making me believe I'm only worth something if I hang a degree

on a wall in a house that I don't even want people in. I'm so sick of society telling me I'm only worth it if my resume doesn't reek of single motherhood, food stamps, and state insurance. That I'm only worth it if I have a husband to claim me. So instead, I place my degree under my bed like I'm hiding a secret. Out of my sight, out of my head. Until I forget it's there. Until I forget it's there. Until I forget it's there so that I'm able to write the poems until I remember that I'm worth this entire world simply because my heart is beating. Until I remember that my name all on its own is a landmark, a continent, this precious jewel still buried, undiscovered, unclaimed. Worthy of celebration without a wedding ring. Until I remember, I'm Oh Sarah Lee with the fattest ass, and what is better than that? What is better than looking in the mirror and loving who is looking back at me? What is better than knowing that my greatest accomplishments were going back upstairs from my basement that day and forgiving that man who trespassed my body while I was too drunk to remember how to walk? And loving my parents back alive when they didn't know how to love themselves. And isn't that the point of all this anyway? Some days all I am is someone who survived. Doesn't that deserve a special frame? A place on the wall? On the mantle? Maybe, to hold an entire ceremony so the others that survived can be honored too?

15. The best head I ever received was from a woman.

NUMB

You pull up a chair, slice me open,
"She's so pretty. Can I taste?"
You press your face against my rose.
I watch you eat me without savoring me.
Your pain numbs as my juices pool into your mouth.
Your starving tongue takes its hit.
Is my body your only escape?

DIALECT

He drags himself inside, carrying that heavy whiskey tongue. For once, he calls me baby. He actually touches me, I actually smile. Drunkenness is my favorite language that he knows. My ears are excited to hear his voice.

He spills himself all over the house. I don't mind this type of mess. He plays sad music, leaves his clothing where he takes them off. He eats the leftover dinner on the stove as if the day before, he didn't tell me I couldn't cook. As if the day before, he didn't even show up to eat.

He starts to let things out, all those pains living in his head—story by story. My patient ears listen like a small child being nosy in adult conversations. I don't utter a word. Tears slowly drag down his cheeks as if they were meeting his face for the first time.

He tells me about the hate he keeps safe for his father. About all the nights he wished he didn't drink, about his regret for moving me here away from my sisters, about staring at my spine with deep anger while I cried after he called me selfish for not getting the abortion.

He tells me he doesn't really love me that well because he doesn't know how to love women. I laugh at the lie. I laugh to myself, not aloud. God, I wish I could go back and laugh out loud. He meant to say he doesn't really love me because he just doesn't really love me. That's okay.

I tried to get it and started to understand his cruelty is not innate, and he's just housing it like a guest who won't leave, like a father who beats his wife but won't leave her.

I take what I can get, what I can learn about the real him, what piece of him I can love into loving me tomorrow. I've waited all day for this. For his truth to come out. For him to call me anything outside of my first name. For his hands to soften at the knuckles. For his eyes to gently open for the first time, like a newborn.

I will wait again tomorrow.

MOTHERHOOD

Every man I ever loved, I held on to my chest.
Turned myself into a safe haven.
A space they could sneak inside of.
I picked them up
from the rock bottom they were born in.
Became a mirror so they could see
the potential their fathers never exposed.
I taught them how to find the savior
in their solitude.
I son them by accident, picking up
where their mothers left off.
Unconditionally loving them into a man
good enough for the next woman.
Isn't that what mothers do?
Use our love to mold the best piece of art.
Watch it age.
Watch it gain value.
Watch it become someone else's.

MIRROR

My mother asks me why I'm not dating.
She doesn't know I'm in love with a man
who can't love me back.
I don't want to add to her trauma, so I stay quiet.
I don't want to confirm to her programming
that women are made to beg men to love them.
I don't want her to think she gave birth
to a replica of all the women living in her.
I don't want her to think I'm a woman
that needs to love a man to feel something.
I don't want her to know I've been filling up
my empty parts with men.
Parts that I don't know how to name
and don't know how to love.
I don't tell her my journals are full of men
she will never know, faces she will never meet,
bodies that lay me down but aren't strong enough
to stand next to me.

PHILADELPHIA

When I go back home, people ask me, "How was it? How was Philadelphia?" Ashamedly, I don't have a real answer. I don't know what to say. People want to hear about art, music, and food. They ask as I stare into the distance, remembering my aftertaste is still swimming in your mouth.

I come up with metaphors to describe the city without giving you away. "The city didn't coddle me, like those small towns do, how they show you around, welcome you to stay. Philadelphia ain't like most. It didn't show me how to walk, how to crawl, how to chew before you swallow, careful not to choke. It met me where I was. It came to my level. Fed me memory. Fed me isles of streets filled with lovely people looking for the city's heart in men too."

I want to tell them that I'm in love again. I want to tell them how you feel like the safest place outside of my home. I want to tell them how I've never tasted skin so delicate. I want to tell them I didn't need to explore the city; the city explored me, no inch unworshipped. Took me in without question, loved me like it wanted to be remembered like it was aching to be discovered.

But, I can't utter a word about us. I can't tell them you don't know how to love me, and I can't tell them I'm a little too ready and that you're not lost enough to love someone like me.

My voice cracks with unfinished truth, "It was a good time. I'll miss it."

How was Philadelphia? It loved me brutally. Hand on throat, eyes shedding more than just tears. Mouths connecting like the last puzzle piece with two bodies waking to lovemaking. That turned into not knowing whose hands were whose. Turned into not knowing whose heartbeat belonged to who. Turned into "Stay in bed. I'll make coffee." Turned into I always stay in bed knowing you're making coffee without me. It was more than just a memory made. More like a lifetime that ran out of time. Ran out of days and ran out of whatever he had left of himself to give me.

I keep our 12 months together safe, tucked into my journals, stained onto pages that will wither, turn into nothing, and just might be forgotten.

I write-
"It was a good time. I'll miss it."

TRESPASS

My body remembers you while I drive my children to school. I bury my tired nails into the peeling faux leather steering wheel. I play the music loudly to drown your face out of my head. I stare ahead at what seems like an endless highway. I don't blink for miles, so the tears dry quickly when I cry. I journey my thoughts around that night, what happened, and what my mind fights to picture clearly.

My body remembers you when my legs wrap around my lover. Snippet memories flash when I close my eyes. My bones- a bag. One hundred seventy-five pounds of lifeless body that took record of your fingerprints. I bury my tired nails into my lover's back. I play the music loudly to drown your face out of my head. My eyes hold on to the ceiling, and I question why my body holds on to you, why my body just won't let you go. I stare at the white walls until my lover notices I'm trying to forget.

My body remembers you during movie night. I bury my tired nails into my thighs underneath the blanket, a signal to my brain that this isn't the right time to try to remember what happened. This isn't the time to unpack pain. This isn't the time to remember you staring into my un-dilated eyes. I drown you out by writing poems about that night in my notes app, an honor you do not deserve.

HEALING FROM TRESPASS

Bathing has become
a daily funeral

Steam removes your face
from my inner thighs

I drown my skin until your
fingerprints disappear

The machete water cuts
your teeth out of me

I sit and watch you die
I weep until the tub overflows

QUESTIONS FOR THE WOMAN I WAS LASTNIGHT
after Warsan Shire @warsanshire

Did you really think they wouldn't notice?
It's hard to cover it up with perfume.
Even harder when you taste just like it.
Why do you think they always leave you?
You give yourself away before anyone can make an offer.
Why do you do this?
You take the bare minimum in exchange for your body.
Don't you know they can smell it all over you?
You reek of loneliness.
Don't you know your mouth is a loud wound?
You reveal the hurt in you each time your lips
separate from your face.
I know it is not your fault.
You were abandoned by the people
who were supposed to love you.
I know it's not your fault.
You can't tell the difference between people
and a new place to call home.

SUICIDE

The ocean spits me out of her mouth.
I crawl under a palm tree.
A man gives me a coconut full of sangria.
I swallow the suicide attempt and get drunk.
I walk the beaches' sun-boiling sand the
same way I walk through life, with a strut and
chipped shoulder. If I can't die on my terms,
I'll just fuck life until she wants me dead.

RESORTING - A JOURNAL ENTRY
7/05/2021

A woman sits in the sand as her child makes friends with the tide. Her sunglasses try their best to hide her tearful eyes.

A small boy sells crocheted dolls to a tourist couple, probably on their hundredth vacation together. I listen to them argue about what color their kids would like. I listen to the ache in their voices as if they have run out of reasons to stay together.

Women close by complain about their husbands and getting second chances and harsh upbringings and bad cooking and bodies they now hate.

I sit alone while my ears attempt to separate all this noise from the ocean waves kissing the sand and from the tacky resort music.

It rains every day as if the water washes away the residue from people coming and going constantly. People come and go so quickly; I met a man seven times for the first time.

No one is paying attention. Everyone is just getting to the next hour to the next experience without stopping by the water and letting the ocean baptize them into a new beginning.

I ask myself silently, "Do I stop enough? Do I cry under my sunglasses enough? Do I travel with my lover enough? Do I watch my babies play in the ocean as if it isn't their home enough? Do I go to resorts too often that I forget this is a selling scheme for my pain?"

I have pens with your name on them, waiting for me to drain you out of them until I don't have to use resorts and people-watching as an excuse to justify that I, too, am hiding something.

There are places in my body that still hurt, that still carry painful memories that I never learned to forgive. I, too, am running away from a life outside of here. I don't wear sunglasses; my tears have no place to hide. I wear them on my face the way glass wears rain.

I dive into the water so no one can tell the difference between the salt in my eyes from the salt in the sea. So, no one can tell I'm just as lost as they are.

WRITERS BLOCK

I've written seventeen books in my head this week. My mind is an endless novel. My pen can't keep up with all the thoughts swirling alive inside of me.

When people ask, "What have you written lately?" I say, "Nothing, having a bit of writer's block," but it isn't true. It's just a cover-up, so I don't have to talk about the fact that all the poems I've written are still tucked into my temporal lobe, hidden in the seams until I landscape the words into something worth showing off.

I don't have writer's block. Writing is my second language; the kind without sound, a mouth without an opening.

I inscribe myself all over the innocence of pages. No corner untouched. My truth staring back at me, these poems have turned mirror, and suddenly I'm forced to come face to face with myself.

WHERE I KEEP YOU

You carry him in your eyes, don't you?
I can tell by all the baggage.

THERE IS A PLACE THAT EXISTS WHERE I GET TO BE WITH YOU

Many times, I feel I don't know enough words to write poetry.
I don't have enough light or darkness, pain, or pleasure. Then
I wonder about you. Words begin to pour in like a waterfall,
flowing down the sides of a broken mountain, creating a pool of
memories that drown me. The day I decided to send you away, I
was torn between who I was at the moment and who I'd become
after the fact. I couldn't decide which version of myself I was
less afraid of. Trying to pick the best road seemed like life or
death. Part of me wanted to live. The other part already felt dead.
I could wear a rope around my neck forever or kick this chair
down and leave into the place of the brokenhearted. The place
of mothers who have pain tucked into their pockets, searching
for the identity of their lost ones. Having their truth and their
hearts tattooed on their chests. Completely visible so that maybe
someone could save them from their tragedy. I've been silent
over the years. I've been avoiding people and conversations
because if I utter any more words, I'm afraid someone will hear
my cry for you. They will see my truth that I have been hiding.
Brokenness is what I've been carrying. You are the missing piece
of me that I've been aching to get back. I remember writing you
a letter while your heart was beating inside me. Tears and a pen
with black ink that knew my vocabulary. Words never came from
a pen so intense, like that day. Words never came so intense ever
again. I remember being on my knees, having the nerve to ask
God to protect you on the other side, while at the same time,
the pill to erase you from my body sat on the end table. When I
close my eyes, I picture us crossing the street. Yet when I look
back, you're still waiting on the other side with your hands up,
reaching for me. I can't get to you. You can't get to me. Two
different worlds wedged in between us. Yet, I can still feel the
roaring pain from when you left my body. How could it be that
I decided to give you up and still feel like you were taken away
from me? Before a deep flow of reddish rose-like color that was
once your anatomy growing steady flowing out of me, I silently
whispered I love you. I collected my tears and wrote your story on
paper that I carefully pushed into a bottle and placed by the sand

with the hope the ocean would one day return you to me. This newfound life I've given myself is like being thrown into a valley, and I've been sitting here waiting for someone to pull me out. Most nights, I gaze at the stars and beg them to save me from my sins instead of using them as stepping stones to climb out of this realm I've placed myself in. I stole my own heart. I don't know how to put it back. So, I write my feelings down in hopes that someone will eventually notice. Notice that I am looking for you. Notice that I long to touch your skin. The best form of poetry I ever wrote came from the tears I cried for you. There is a place that exists where I get to be with you. I just hope it's everything I imagine it to be.

BUKOWSKI AND A LOVE THAT ISN'T READY

You buy me the best of Bukowski. Then later, after eating my pussy for 20 min, you tell me you're unsure of me.

I swallow my pride like a shot of whiskey you're peer-pressured into taking, almost spitting it out, too sharp with loud truth, too much for a voice that can't stick up for itself.

You don't look up at me when I ask, "So, what are we then?" Your tongue swells with words too big for your mouth. Vocabulary flies out of you, looking for an audience to convince, and I realize you don't know the answer.

You say you aren't ready for a relationship; you bring up so many things to validate your un-want for me. Like, I don't believe in your God. Yet, you just fucked the God in me, like I'm saving you from all your sins. And I want to cry like I do when I'm alone.

I hear you out. Hear your excuses for dragging this year on. I hear you tell me you can't love me because I'm just a little too much, I'm just a little too head of household, I'm just a little too independent, I'm just a little too in my own lane.

All my ears grasp onto is that you can't love a woman that doesn't know fear. You can't love a woman who knows what she wants and isn't afraid to burn down cities to find it. All I can see is that you can't love a woman who thinks God looks like her.

FOR NOW

The chicken fries to a crisp,
sweat slides down your face.
The record player in the living room
isn't very loud,
we dance to all the love songs anyway.
It's the peak of summer,
the heat has nowhere to go,
it floats on top of the concrete and skin.
The AC window unit fights hard to cool
the house down, but this kitchen is
swollen with mid-July and grease.
You grab my sweltering waistline
and force your hand up my skirt for the 10th time today.
You pull out what you need, lick your fingers,
and kiss my mouth.
I wish you would reach in me for something deeper.
I know you're not in love with me.
I know your kind.
I've swallowed men like you.
Men who know women like me
have pussy that makes a better man.
That's all you're really looking for, aren't you?
A healer, a void filler, some good ass to ease all your regrets.
But you don't want to keep me.
You aren't fooling anyone.
And my abandonment issues like how this feels, for now.
I'll take the days back when it's time.
I'll take back what's mine in time.
"The chicken is ready!"

THE POISON IN MY TRUTH

When we first met, you looked at me with accomplished pupils,
like I was the body of water that fit perfectly into your mouth.
I knew you were thirsty. And hungry. And needed to be filled.
I saw you looking at me in the glass reflection. Like my first name
was take it. Like you knew, your hands would be wrapped around
my neck sooner than later.

You blew your cover when you touched my lower back in passing.
You were testing me, figuring me out, silently warming me up.
But baby, I'm a scholar. One thing I read more than books is
people. I could feel you wanted to teach me some new shit. Some
grown shit. Some show me how much you can handle shit. But
this ain't my first time running.

Did you think I hadn't been here? In a place where nothing really
matters. Not even the naked body next to you, because tomorrow
it will be gone anyway. You should've known by the arch in my
back that I've done this a time or two.

When you landed your face onto the tender valley of my
inner thighs, I knew you were a writer. A poet in your own way.
A creator licking the inspiration out of me. A hunter in the way
you moved your tongue so swiftly. As if you've been looking for
women like me. Women who know how much of a shapeshifter
they can become in the bedroom. The kind of woman who
resembles a rest stop, where you can take the time to unwind
because those empty spaces in you keep your mind racing.

Did you think I haven't had good dick before? Do you think
you're the first to try to outperform the rest? Come up with
something better. Get my bones to move in a way that I'm
desperate to run back to you. You are so easy on the eyes, my
love, and women who aren't like me are so fooled by it. And to
be honest, I don't care how many times you thought of filling me
up to the breaking point. I have places living in me you will need
more than dick to get to.

You remind me of me. Slick with the shit. A cold piece of work. A good person who does bad things sometimes. The difference is I can fake it better. I'm sorry you were unable to tell the difference. But I guess an ass like this will do that to a man.

When you asked me whose pussy this belonged to, I lied and said it was yours because the empty part of me wanted to belong to someone for once, even if it was just the hollow of me. I lied so well I almost believed myself.

And you slept like a kite on a windy day when we finished with such ease. And I know you didn't tell me to leave. But you didn't ask me to stay either. So, I left you unawakened and uncovered. And with the hope that maybe one day we can be naked for once without being naked for once.

STORAGE

The slit between my legs, -a fragile cabinet,
safely keeps your memory alive in me.
My tired fingers, looking for you,
dig inside until they find your hiding spot.
"There you are," I whisper to myself.
I pull your face out and wear you
on my fingers like rings.
Licking your memory clean off,
I close my eyes and savor you,
in my mouth- a drawer,
another place I keep you safe.

DESTRUCTION

I knew you weren't good for me,
I longed for you.

I knew you had poison on your skin,
I wanted to taste you.

I knew you could cause hurt,
I wanted to feel pain by you.

You are a destruction.
Destroy me.

III

I am constantly searching for you because when I find
you I find me

UNTITLED

My love,
I wont wait around for you.
But I will drag my feet into the sand,
incase you ever go looking for me.

FOR MARCELLINO 1964-2018

I sit on the ledge of my grief, looking out unto the silk sky carrying the moon. I puzzle together the constellations until they bring me your face. I imagine you up there, making the stars fall in love with you. I think about the gods and how jealous they must have gotten when they heard you were making your grand appearance.

These days I find myself decorating the poems I wrote for you with my tears. The words do get old, but the pain of your loss is still younger than the morning.

Some days I wonder if my grief is heavy enough to hold me down if I jumped. I'm not sure how much longer I can pretend she doesn't exist. She's beginning to gain weight, and one day she will snag a button or snag my life.

When my thoughts get loud like this, I think about your tattooed skin. When it rains, I pretend it's your hands making their way to comfort me. When I write, you always fall from my pen, creating a way to keep you alive.

I cry silently to myself at night to not wake the worry out of my children. There is no patient sunrise that compares to the time I wait for you to find me in my dreams.

This burning river below my dangling feet could take all this pain away, yet it doesn't guarantee I'll see you again. So instead, I've made a home out of your absence, and you know me, I don't like going places. So, I've been here for a while, begging time to bring you back to me.

I can't even visit your grave because it forces me to make friends with the truth. I'm still waiting to mourn your voice. I'm afraid it will mean our memories together will slip from my fingertips.

I try to sort through my tangled emotions to find the one to get me through the day, yet each day seems like a death I'm forced to attend without a chance to rest in peace. Are you resting in peace?

In my dreams, you and I aren't carrying expectations on our backs; it's just us. It's just you, forgiving me for not forgiving you while your heartbeat was a melody and not just a memory.

So, I'll sit here on the ledge of my grief, looking out unto the silk sky carrying you.

YOU ARE TO ME WHAT FOOD IS TO THE HUNGRY

My ears are starving
to hear my name race
from your tongue.
Out of anger or joy,
I need to be fed
your voice again.

BREAKING

It rained like Mother Earth baptized the whole city that night. Not a sin left untouched. She must've known you lied when you told me you'd be out of town a few days. She must've known you were talking about another woman, not another city.

It was 12 AM, late enough for me to find a cold alley to die in. Late enough for me to go out into the water and get lost. Instead, I waited in the car until the sky gave me the okay to get out. I walked into the empty house, rarely greeted with a smile, let alone your presence. I laid down our children in bed, put myself into bed alone. Again, another night of you missing. Again, another night of me sticking around, not listening to the signs to leave you. I checked my phone a hundred times, still nothing from you, not even a "fuck you."

I should've stood out in the rain. Let Mother Earth slaughter you out of me, gut me clean of your trespassing hands. I should've let her set me and the city free from sinning lovers looking for escapes in wounded people like they don't need saving too.

Maybe if I let the rain take you from my blood, you would want to come home for once. Nickname me, Los Angeles; take a tour of me, find some hidden gems in me that you can't see on my face. Isn't that what you do? Crawl into different women, each from a different city, pretending to show them something different about you, but the only difference about you is all the different women. I know each of them. Their scent holds onto our bed sheets. Their pain clings to my hair. I can hear their voices in my head.

Don't you know you carry them back home each time? This house is full of wounded women attempting to save a wounded man. Even Mother Earth shows up - with all this rain.

I WILL ALWAYS AND NEVER HAVE YOU

You stained me like a memory. Cut into me like a sun ray through silk cloud. Gave me a pain only a drought could bring.

I tuck our infidelity under the truth, place the pictures of her under your sink. We do not exist in the reality of those who know us, and soon your place will shake loose of my DNA.

The comfort of your bed won't feel me any longer. But I will remember us, and you will remember us, and the moon, she will remember us.

How we begged her to stay awake just a little longer, to vacate from our truth, empty ourselves into one another. Make love as if though we were lovers.

But my body knows no lies. My body knew you were not meant to stay here. It is no wonder why I began missing you so soon.

I despise a love that imitates the seasons, leaves, and returns. The leaving always lasts longer. This relationship is a burning flame in my stomach, and as real as fire is, you could never love me.

So let there be space between your memory and your touch because lies age fast, to the point that you forget them.

She can never know about me. About the days I planted sunflowers in your belly, so the sun could always take you back to the root of you and I.

This lie between us is getting heavy. The bags underneath my eyes show exactly where I carry you. And your eyes show exactly where you carry her.

That thing that eats you will never go away until you're exhausted from feeding it, and I am running out of days. My body is repenting you, and like confession, there is consequence.

The woman who calls you her lover doesn't know me from Adam or rumor and isn't that the scariest part? I could look her dead in the face and know exactly who she is. And I? Just a stranger.

The gargoyles that watched us on the edges of our sky-scraping lies know what we deserve, and it isn't each other.

As bad as I want to stay, I cannot make a home out of a home already built by another woman's love.

I will always and never have you. Like a carcass, you can touch it, but dead is dead, and that is where pain makes a home for me.

LISTEN

after Alexis Briones @xobriones

Listen,
You a horizon of a woman,
endless breathtaking of a sunset.
They come by the thousands to witness your beauty.

Listen,
You a continent of a woman,
a canvas for earth.
Men travel outside of here,
just to look at you from a star's point of view.

Listen, Woman,
you a city at night,
acquainted with experience,
stretched by broken promises.
Few can see old bruises sleeping in your eyes.
Few brave enough to dive into you. Few can keep up.

Listen, Woman,
You a cheat code to this life.
Don't let them tell you any different.
You a prayer on a hot day.

Listen, Woman,
You are the thing that saves us all.
You are the thing that saves us all.

ON WRITING WHEN I COULD NOT

I want to write, but I don't have a thing to say. I want to say something inspiring or motivating or exciting. I want to tell a story about rising to the occasion when I didn't have an ounce of happiness in me. I want to talk about me. But I always talk about me. And I always talk about love. And I always talk about being in love. And I always talk about what I would do if love found me again. But maybe that's exactly what I'm supposed to be writing. Maybe I'm supposed to remind people about love, how it saves us, and how it's only ever supposed to save us. Maybe I'm supposed to be writing about this for all of us. Even me, who sometimes forgets she's so fucking powerful and that love is looking for me. That love is always looking for me.

SUNDAY IN MEXICO

My body submerges into what feels like an ice-filled tub. Goosebumps birth themselves on my skin. My toes push against the blue tile. My head breaks itself eagerly out from the ceiling of the water. You say, "Oh, come on. It's not that cold!" You jump in, "Oh damn, it is cold!" We laugh.

This is my second time with you, and I don't know how many more hours we have left. I don't know how long this timeline lasts. I always think further than I should. Hoping for five thousand years. Hoping never to lose sight of what's right here right now. I'm always imagining and always planting pictures into my head. Like white linen hugging our skin as we read books, our hands never letting go, our mouths exchanging passion before the sun wakes, our tender bodies bleeding into each other to become one, and you making love to me that changes my genetic makeup.

I snap out of daydreaming when you randomly get out of the pool. I swim towards the ledge to look over the view of the city, and I whisper to myself, "You only have to remember the small details, and you'll never forget it." I see the greenery of plants, a chipping-pink-faded building, women clasping hands, a blue patient sky, a bluer ocean, and men starting a fire for the fresh-skinned goat. Those snapshot details stain me. I'll never forget the view. I'll never forget the absolute blue of this day. I'll never forget the air licking my skin warm in the pool.

I place my hands on the sun-kissed ledge and push my body out of the crisp water to peek over the rooftop pool. I look back to find you standing tall, water dancing off your skin like a night full of confident stars. You take pictures of me, and I tell myself, "He won't ever forget this view. He will never look at this city and not see my vastness all over it."

OUT OF BODY
after Lucille Clifton

Listen with your eyes, I beg of you.
All my letters at your door, sealed with hope.
See the strands of my hair sprinkled in your home,
curved with so much question. Can you hear them?
In your sink, hiding in the carpet, singing out to you
like women in a choir, one by one, then all at once.
Can you feel me looking for you?
This is the only language I can speak to you in,
my tongue is exhausted.
I'm trying to tell you I'm still in love with you.
I'm trying to tell you,
I'm still in love with you.

LOVE IS THE ACT

There was a small moment
when my voice wanted to whisper,
"I love you."
Hadn't known you longer
then a season of summer.
Not sure if my eyes will ever
have another chance to look
into yours or if we will ever
be under the same full moon
in the same city again.
Isn't that the point of love?
To be present, to give it freely,
to have the courage to say
"I love you" when it rises
to the occasion.
To wish you a kinder winter
with the horizon of my body
pushed up eagerly against yours.
To kiss your spine passionately
while touching your tattooed skin.
To rub the heels of your tender feet
as you wish, so after your long days
when I am not there to soothe the pain
the thought of my touch calms you.
Isn't that love already in itself?
The things that we do, the act,
the giving and being okay
without getting anything in return?
I don't know why I couldn't muster up
the courage to say it.
Maybe that's exactly what you needed to hear.
Who's to say you aren't deserving?
When I sit with the memory of loving you
I can still hear the breeze through
the curtains of your bedroom.
I can still feel your legs

intertwined with mine.
Your voice takes over all the rooms I walk into
because I can still hear you in my head.
Is this not love already in itself?
Is it not love that I would break
into pieces for you so you can taste me a hundred ways?
Love found me again underneath you
just when I thought it had given up on me.
Thought love didn't know how
to make its back home in me.
In that small moment, you were mine,
and I was yours, and you held me
like tomorrow wasn't coming to save us.
We did it all, but we didn't have
the courage to say it, so here I'm going to say it,
I love you.
I loved you then. I love you now.
I'll love you always in yesterday's memory.

FORGET

He makes love to me
like it's the last time, every time.
I tell him I've been waiting
all my life for his touch.
He pries my knees open
I welcome him home.
I make him forget
about all the times
he entered into someone
that wasn't me.

TURBULANCE

Flight attendants hand out drinks, and I prepare my exhausted voice to make a proper decision. "What do you want?" In this case, it's peanuts or crackers. Water or Sprite. Just two hours ago, you were stumbling over the same question. And like a new poet, you searched for the right words to not offend your listener by soothing the awkward space between us with half-truths of loving me fully one day when you're ready. But I know what you meant to say. You can't love a woman who uses her tongue for more than just pleasing ears and sucking dick. You can't love a woman who's shapeless, uncontrollable, undominated, like turbulence.

I pull my Texas orange hoodie over my face as a signal. No one on a plane bother's someone like that. Besides, I can't tell if I want a drink or a conversation with someone who will listen to my body purge you out. Either would wash down the aftertaste of a good cry. Which reminds me of all the times I held my truth hostage behind my teeth. Clenching it shut, so I don't miss out on being chosen by you. My body has done everything to keep you. Even if it meant betraying myself.

How many hoodies will I use as a cloak to cover your lack of love on my face? How many planes rides? How many miles will it take for my body set you free? It's hard to accept that the problem here is me. I'm the unmanageable thing that knocks fear out of men and asks them to dance. And how does a man carry such a thing? How can a man love an unconquerable woman? How can I make you choose between your unreadiness and this woman who, like turbulence, isn't afraid of anything?

ON COMMAND

I'm no longer
in love with him.
Yet the thought
that continues to sit
in my eyes, is not
how we were in love,
but the way I loved him.
My heart wrestles
with the memory
of how he would tell
my body to break
into pieces
and it would listen.
Every.
Single.
Time.

LOSS

I've lost years of my life searching for where I stand in yours.

FULL OF YOU

I eat at the idea of you coming back,
taking bites too big to chew.
I swallow memories of us whole.
I want to feel you moving around in me.
Maybe this way you will stay.
Maybe this way, you will fill me up a bit longer.

I eat until I cannot breathe.

VOIDS

I touch myself as I miss you,
reaching inside a void
for an emotion I can feel.

There is something ready
to expel from my insides,
I feel it pulsating,
I massage it slowly.

I scroll through
all the videos of us together,
trying to master it out
from between my legs
and it's clear
I need more than an orgasm.

I tried to push it out,
tried to get whatever it is
off under the sheets.

I can still feel it hiding me,
still clawing at my insides,
still pregnant with the waiting,
barricaded in my rib cage.

I should make use of this vacancy,
but with what? A body? My hands?
A man? A pathetic excuse for a lover?
All will fit, and none will stay.

How should I rid myself of this unoccupied empty?

AFTER THE WOUNDS CLOSE UP

There is a life I once lived.
My harsh life,
a sea without a sun
a shipwreck doused in lovers.

Where do I go
after I've rinsed myself
of the harsh seasons?
Wrote out the hurt
shouted out the mountain of tears.

Who am I today?
Is there really a difference?
Am I two different women?
Am I outgrowing old bones?

Is this what healing feels like?
Looking for myself in old journals
unable to picture my own face
unable to remember my own touch.

Who do I fill myself back up with?
This version of me I have yet to write down
I don't know where the hurt lives
I don't know these poems yet.

When all the women you've tried to become
climb out of you to breathe
Do you place them back into the scar tissue?
Do you get a new version of yourself if they leave for good?

Where do you go when you've gone
to all the places that have called your name?
When you undressed the programs and conditions?
Where do you go when you've faced yourself?

I have cut out the gods in me from my hips,
set the generations stuck in my ache, free.
Forgave myself for all the times
I did not choose myself.

This is for all the days I didn't know love
for the girl who cracked in half,
setting all the women housed in me free.

After the wounds close up, where must I go?
Who must I turn myself into?
Which woman do I want to become?

ACHE

It's been nine months since my eyes analyzed your face.
The consequence of loving you had its way with me, and
I still can't tell the difference between a bruise and a poem.
I've been mistaking sadness for love again.
And I thought I healed those empty spaces in me.
I guess my body still thinks it needs a man to fill it.
Needs a man to patch up the holes. Needs you.

MUSCLE MEMORY

I haven't had a chance to forget you.
Haven't had a chance to look at myself
in the mirror to face the parts that look like you.
It's been weeks since I've written about you.
The longer I wait, the louder your voice gets in my head.

I need to drain you out of me. I need to cry you out of me,
I need to pen you down.
You must've known love is revealing.
You must've known love opens the hiding spaces underneath the
patched-up ache.

Is that why you let me go?
Did I wake up the memories in your muscle? The ones you forced
your body to forget,
to silence, to cover up with lies that keep you safe from the
demons in your bloodline.

When did you know you couldn't love me?
When did you figure out I wasn't scared of heartbreak?
Can you hear my silhouette looking for you still?
Can you feel my body holding space for all that you are? All that
you come with, all the lies and brutal truths.

My skin wants to manifest your tongue back.
My body is looking for you.

Give me something to feel again, to hold in me for keepsake,
even if it's tender at the touch, even if it hurts.

GIVE A WOMAN WHAT SHE WANTS

You send music to my phone
Lyrics panting with hope
Inflated with the regret of losing me
My insides curl up
The room goes quiet.

I listen to the song again and again
Touch myself after
Pleasure doesn't replace love
It can't outdo the year we spent together.

Bobby Womack sings about losing his lover
"Give a woman what she wants," he says
He doesn't leave footnotes on how to do just that.

Did your father ever run after your mother?
Did he ever give her more than a playlist
to read between the lines in the chorus?
Did he ever put down the ego, put down some tears,
go after his woman and give her what she wants?
Do you know what a man in love looks like?

I can only think of the times
I clawed onto something I knew
I couldn't afford to lose
Ran out of tears
Gave up my god
Left my hometown
all for love.

You send music that says a lot
You say so little
I pretend I can't hear you.

So you can call my phone
Pull up in my city

Trace me down
Get me back.

IN ANOTHER LIFE
part I

In another life, I sit in a coffee shop writing poetry, trying to hold back my tears. The man next to me, who probably has a good wife at home, has been staring at the way my legs are tightening as I write. He offers to buy me coffee. Then lunch. Then his mouth. And I accept it. God did I, and God did I die in his mouth, and God did he spit me back out a new woman.

He doesn't know I'm aching with the memory of you. He doesn't know that as his mouth kissed the rose of my inner thighs, I imagined it was your mouth. I imagined it was your eyes cutting me out of the room. I imagined it was your hands holding me at the arch of my back. And it was you. And I will not accept any other version of the story. It was your tongue I melted on through him, even if I had to close my eyes to make it real.

In another life, that baby is ours. She has your lips and my eyes. We name her after the city we first met in, and she's tall like you. She has my slick mouth and understanding heart. We watch her grow together. We teach her music. All the good shit, you know. We show her the truth of life and never force her to be who she doesn't want to become. She teaches us how to love each other better. She teaches us how to love. She teaches us that no matter how far we drift from one another, we are always together in her. In another life, I move to a town where I cook for a living. I have my plants, my books, the ocean, and no children. I don't know shit about anything but my small town. I'm okay, I'm happy, and I don't want to run away to the next city to be saved from a life that has hardened me from the inside. I only know simple things. I only know pleasurable touch, good-tasting food, dancing women, and the moon's light. I only know how to take care of myself. It is the only life I ever only know how to just take care of myself.
In another life, you stay.
In another life, I don't leave.

FEAST WITH OUR BODIES ON THE TABLE
after Alysia Nicole Harris @poppyinthewheat

We smelled like the fresh coming of age
Ate takeout and danced
like birds of paradise calling in their mate.
Our sacred bodies, fenced in by religion,
couldn't tell the difference between love and lust.
We each shaved our inner thighs.
We were told they looked best that way.
We listened with sharp ears and aching throats.
It felt good to be chosen,
even if the chooser swallowed the innocence out of our faces.
It felt good to be wanted,
even if the wanter's pupils had no hint of staying.
We didn't know. We were young with empty swollen hips
like churches taking in beggars, and we believed we could save
them.
No one told us sex appeal meant two things; attention-whore
and used.
No one told us when our bodies are greeted with a man's mouth;
we are tainted and unwanted by the rest.
No one told us our thighs opened or closed had the same fate.
We were young and full of the heat of marriage and babies and
for any of those young men to return, if maybe, for life.
We were devoured and left bones and made to believe this was a
woman's destiny.

IV

I inhale all of you then exhale poems

DREAM

You are a dream.
I think that's all you're
supposed to be.

HONEST WORK

I

Truth is, you got the absolute worst of me. There was nothing about me then that I go back to look for. There was an empty well in my abdomen that could never be filled as much as you tried. You got the cruel Sarah. The version of myself I no longer have contact with. I do not know her. I do still love her. But I do not know her. Truth is, when I write, you still come out to find me. You spill from my pen and still love the worst parts of me in these pages.

II

Truth is, I take inventory of all my regrets in my belly and labor the metaphors when they are ready to crawl out of me. Truth is, I don't mind giving birth to painful poems. I do mind when they make an unrepairable mess out of me that I don't speak for days. I do mind when the margins are too wide. They get stuck and die inside of me. Truth is, sometimes the pain is so brutal I can't write for weeks. I run short on tears and ink. I run short on who I say I am and hide from myself.

III

Truth is, poetry makes a mess out of me. Spreads me open, enters me but does not pull out. Calls me home. Calls me darling. Truth is, poetry makes me submit, on my knees, begging to be emptied. The truth is poetry has a grip on me that I cannot outrun. Her weight lays me down and picks me up. Truth is, poetry is the map that has led me back home to myself.

EGO DEATH

Bury the old you.
Bury her deep into the ground.
I've buried the old me a hundred times.
My backyard is full of the casualties of my old self.

A LOVE LETTER TO MYSELF

You are the blue
that turns into deeper blue once opened.
I can always find you where the ocean
and the sky hold each other.

And your feet, the way they lead you
to every place that calls for you.
Each serving its purpose.
Each belonging to all the parts of you.
The way wind belongs to the wings of a bird.
The way attention finds you each time you speak.

Anyone that is lucky enough to cross your path
stops and stares at you like road trip scenery.
Looking at the distance of you every time
and still finding something new to appreciate.

Sometimes that's all I'm given - the present
moment of your face. I so lucky to have
been given eyes that trust me enough.
I am honored to receive so much beauty all at once.

You unwarranted storm with rainbows after,
you are chaos and peace.
Both times, you are beautiful.
Both times, I am still and watch you.
Both times, I love you.

HOME
for Julia

I can rewrite this all, rewrite this life,
just say the word. I'm at your command.

I can take away the caving floor,
take away the bunk beds,
give you a room you're in love with.

I can take the church walls down,
take away the pressuring eyes,
give you an empty landscape as a stage to sing.

I can make them leave you alone,
take away their voices,
give you a reason to laugh.

I can make Grandpa come back,
have him pick you up in the apple red van
and let him sing you his Spanish songs.
I can give you one more Sunday with him,
if you asked.

I can turn our little green house into a mansion,
we can laugh as loud as we want,
we can sneak out without getting caught.

I can write you into any life you want,
give you the rest you deserve,
give you uninterrupted motherhood,
give you the time back you spent helping
raise Adriana.

But what I cannot do,
is call you by another name,
turn you into someone else.

What I cannot do

is place you elsewhere in the world,
change your face, change your location.
I still need you even when I don't.

I cannot look at you and not see my home.
I cannot look at you and not see my savior.
I cannot look at you and not see my daughter's other mother.

Maybe we did it right the first time.
Maybe I don't have to make changes.
Maybe we aren't alone after all.
Maybe, just maybe, we always needed each other.
Maybe, after all, we survived this life.
Maybe, after all, we did it right.

I WILL CHOOSE LOVE

Even when the warmth of the sun
stops setting foot in my home,
Even when the hands of hate behead Cupid.
I will curl myself into a weeping rainfall,
reveal the begging bones of old lovers,
turn myself into love's soldier,
conjure up the dead poets as an army,
slice the horizon down its center,
demand the sky to bleed forgiveness
into the cracks of every unfaithful mountain.
I'll turn myself into dust,
become love's soil, birth unfurling roses
watch the roots play fire as they spread into the vastness.
I'll be the singing red bird,
that forces you to look up and be still.
I'll be a mirror,
that reflects the sunset each time you
forget love already lives in you.
I'll be the ocean,
kissing the land over and over again.
Just for you to sit and listen, sit and remember.
And I will not rest.
I will choose love.
Even after these pages turn scratch paper.
Even after, no one remembers my name.
I will choose love.
Even if I have to become it.

ARCHEOLOGISTS FIND THE TOMB OF WAHTYE THAT IS 4,500 YEARS OLD

I bury all the poems I've ever written in my front yard. You're in there, waiting to be found like you've been waiting your entire life. One day someone will unearth you. You will be reborn again. Someone will rush to sleep just to rush to wake to keep learning about you. To read the words written about you, to understand you better, to remember you, and bring you back to life.

No one has forgotten you. You are written on every single page. You have been resting and growing in all directions. Someone will stop right here and feel you calling their name. They won't stop searching until they find you. They will turn over every stone with bare hands. They will open the ground to find you as beautiful as ever and say, "She's been here the whole time!"

Someone's coming to wake you out of a death you have been longing to resurrect from. Longing to climb out of. They are coming by the hundreds. Everyone will soon know your name. Sometimes it takes 4,500 years to remember a soul like yours. Sometimes it takes forty men to unearth your being to shake the entire world.

And when they do, they will hold you over their heads. They will bow at your feet. They will read every single page you've ever written and tell every set of eyes they come across about your language, your power, and your life.

You will rise again. All those poems you've ever written will be someone's bible.

You won't go another day without being praised.

YOU

There is a massacre that happens
inside of my body
when the memory of you
makes its way into my head.

I weed out the noise
with different bodies.
Lovers that die out the pain.
Each a replica of you,
crawling in and out of me.

The night finds me.
The moon watches
through my bedroom window.
I see your face looking at me.
I can taste the difference between you
and all the men I shelter myself under.

They don't love me like you.
They can't love me like you.
No one can love me so brutally like you.

QUESTIONS FOR THE MAN I WAS WITH LASTNIGHT

When you told me I was beautiful, did you mean the way my lips made you think about fucking me? Or did you mean the sunrise that my poetry reminds you of?

Do you think about my empty spaces, what happened, and why I haven't filled them back up? Or do you only think about filling me up with the little that you do have?

Do you think about my body and the battles it put up with between giving birth and all the times it tensed up when men made an object out of it? Or did you only think about how it would look so good naked on top of yours?

Do you think about how loving me would feel like freedom? Or how listening to my voice read to you sounds like peace?

Do you ever wonder what else there is to me besides knowing what position I like? Or how I like my hair pulled? Did you know that I am a whole universe with galaxies, with my own constellations, my own north star, my own mystery? That, yes, some have figured out, but never stayed long enough to see where I keep all my pain hidden.

Do you even know how to land on my heart? Do you know how to read the map of my skin? Do you know how to find the clit of my mind? Or do you just think about cumming and going like the rest of them did?

Or maybe you do know I am what I am, and you're afraid to get lost like the others who just weren't enough to stick around and left as soon as it started to get dark. It's easy to fall in love with my body, but you can't love me if you didn't notice all my convictions doing time in my pupils.

Did you even notice? Or did you just notice how good I probably taste, how nice I probably do look on my knees? It's a sight to see, you know, to be honest.

The best of me isn't my mouth or my skin. I get wetter when one takes the time to fuck me with their mind, teach me something no one else has the balls enough to do. But no one wants to dig around and see what's died in me.

They're afraid because I know exactly what I want and how to get it. How I wake up before my alarm clock because someone decided to put a measurement on time, so I'm racing myself against it. They're afraid of a woman who isn't scared to be herself, who talks about sex and how yea I do like my shit yanked after a night of opening my wounds and explaining I still don't know shit about life but the day, and that's okay because I'm fighting for myself.

They're afraid of the poison in my truth. They're afraid of loving someone who isn't scared of herself, who isn't afraid to use the stage of her pain to show people this is where you find who you are.

Are you ready for the home in me that has seen un-homey shit? That has housed undeserving lovers that has let in too much hurt. I refuse to lease the empty parts of me to those who don't want to stay for life anymore.

Do you still think I'm beautiful?

IN ANOTHER LIFE
part II

In another life, he leaves me for another woman
who's younger, prettier, and shuts her mouth when told to.
He tells me that he doesn't love me anymore.
He tells me, "I don't want you anymore, Sarah."

My knees introduce themselves to the floor,
to prove that my bigness can fold into itself.
To prove he doesn't have to find a new woman,
that I could shape-shift into a quiet moon,
if that's what he wanted.

I look up at him like a tall building standing over me.
He tells me that maybe down the road, we can try again.
He walks out of my front door for the last time.
My 3-year-old son sits with me until my eyes grow
tired from crying. I get up and make dinner.

In another life, I fuck a few men to relieve
the sting of loneliness, and none of them noticed.
Some men don't know a life without a woman
pouring herself into them. They've only ever known
a woman to be half-dead. The kind of woman that
resembles their mother, who was forced to give
up her body in exchange for love.

And I don't blame them for not noticing.
No one teaches them how to take care of a woman.
They only teach them how a woman must take
care of them. I only blame them for attempting to
take ownership of this vacant house. I was never looking
to be owned. I was just looking for someone to vacation
with at two in the morning during secret-telling to get
away from the dead spaces living in me that
no one leaves flowers for.

In another life, I leave the church and tell all the priests

to fuck off. I tell Jesus I'm no longer filling my throat
with his flesh. I will no longer get on my knees and
ask a man to forgive me for sins I enjoyed committing.
I will no longer get on my knees and teach my children
that God is a man when they've only ever witnessed
men leaving and only ever witnessed women making
miracles out of food stamps and negative bank accounts.
When they've only ever witnessed their mother die
every night and rise from the dead in the morning.

In another life, I don't care if you can't love me.
I just write more often. I don't stop writing.
I never stop writing.

A BAD POEM

He will never quite get it; how to love an open wound like
you. And after you, he will try to cut women open, looking for
the passion your blood gives. He will never find the thing that
sutured his empty parts like you.

She's the mask, the perception, the cover-up from the real
woman he wants to take home to his mother and say, "Look, I
love her, and you can't do shit about it."

She's on her knees, trying her hardest to keep her lipstick nice
while giving him head. And you know, with me, he gets on his
knees first, pries me open, tastes me, takes me, empties me, and
makes love to me in the morning after I've gotten some sleep
because he likes the idea of touching my body before sunlight
does.

She's horseback riding in one of those stupid suits, and
I'm the type of woman who's talked about in a bar earning
invisible trophies for being the baddest bitch to ever do it.
She's generational wealth, and I come from too many kids and
unhealed trauma. The difference between her and me is that I
have nothing to lose. I'm a California fire, and she's the grass that
can't keep up. And he knows it. He feels it in his bones.

He will always stare at books and see my face. He can't hear a
storm and not hear my voice. He knows I uncover all his hiding
spots. He can't outrun me. He can't outrun the truth.

I don't know what it's like to settle for the safe thing that makes
you look good when others look at you. I don't know what it's like
to pick the safe lover. I don't know what it's like not to love the
Tsunami in someone.

HUMAN

Many things in life tried to kill me.
Myself included.
Call it treason.
Come up with excuses.
Make it sound valid.
Make it understandable.

Some of us confuse dying and living.
Weeping sounds like laughter.
Mirrors look like windows.
The ocean smells like the sky.
It all looks the same!

How can I know something
if I can't see it wholly?
How can I love something
if I don't know it wholly?
Myself included.

The most human thing
some of us know is a death
you don't die from.
The most human thing
some of us know is a life
you don't know how to live.

O I LOVE YOU
for the women of poems and integrity

There are corpses piled up across the river
Clogging it like an artery
All the bodies
Different lifetimes
Different versions
All the same woman
All me

I've died many times
Still got up in the morning
Placed the casualties of me in the water
With hope, they are carried to a new life,
to a different feeling
Less painful
Less swollen with grief
Less heavy with the waiting

Today I decided to lay my old live's to rest
Pull them out of hells waiting room
Give each a proper burial
Give each an altar for a headstone

The first body;
Heartbroken
Back bent too far
Knees covered in blood
Never knew the sun was born from her eyes

The second body;
Gave birth too young
Only knew harsh seasons
Only knew winter for a mother

The third body;
Colonized by rape
Taken into a room

Didn't leave the same woman
Swallowed pain
Hid it in her belly
Never let it out
Never realized there was a way out

Each body doused with stories
Drenched with unnoticed poems
Covered in books, unread

Lifetimes of me clogging my destiny
Clogging this unforgiven river
I want to let go
I want to mourn the dead spaces made up of me
I didn't know that when you're doing the dying
You can still hear your old voices
Begging to be loved

I go for the fourth body
Raise my right hand over my patient eyebrows
Claps my drooping mouth with my left
There are more bodies now
This time not dead
This time not me
This time there are women
Singing, "O, I love you, O, I love you."
Carrying old versions of me to the graveyard
Holding the old bodies of me the way I did not hold myself
As if my past lives were daughters, they never stopped loving

Each woman lay poems on my bodies
Like roses on caskets
And altogether, they sing me back alive
They sing me back alive

MY LIFE

Poems fall out of your pen like running water
You write every single day without it hurting
You publish the book
About all the lovers
About all the heartbreak
About all the times you did not choose yourself,
You meet so many people that love your words
You change them, and they change you
Your poems travel all over the world
They sit on shelves in cities you've never heard of
They hang on walls in living rooms you will never step into
You move out of Kansas, finally
You aren't scared anymore
You buy the beach house that sits on sand as soft as silk
You wake up early to meditate in the ocean and shout
"This is my life!"
You fill the house with all the plants you saved from clearance
racks
You name each of them after a goddess
You drink tea every day instead of coffee
Your family comes to visit every summer
Dad still is never satisfied
He roams around the house looking for things to fix
He still wants you to need him,
but he doesn't know that you will always need him
He tells you he's proud of you and that he's writing again
He makes a fire pit on the beach
You write affirmations together, then burn them
This will be his first of many magic spells, and he's finally okay
with you being a bruja
You and your kids get matching tattoos that say, "You're Mine"
Your daughter still calls you every day
Your son still reaches for your hair
You have an amazing relationship with your kids, the kind you
wish you had with your parents
The man you wrote so many poems about still thinks about you

He will never stop thinking about you
He will still call you to make sure you still love him even though
he is married now and had another baby
You two laugh about all the memories you have together, good
and bad
He tells you he will find you again in the next life
Maybe not as lovers, but maybe he will be a bird and you a tree
Still needing you to love him some way some how
You get married
Your husband builds you a sunroom and a library
And he never complains about all the plants or that you're
running out of space
He just builds you a greenhouse
He's madly in love with you
He loses control when you're half-naked in front of him
He can't keep his hands off you
This you love the most about him
The way he makes an altar out of you with his fingertips
He leaves you love notes in between pages of books for you to
find
You're always so surprised and so happy when you find a new one
You take mom to Brazil
She cries the whole way there
She never knew poetry could take you across the world
She mails you letters, and you keep each one
Her handwriting is still perfect
You will grow very old
You will die peacefully
But before you go
You publish another book
About love
About heartbreak
About singing the god in you alive
About orgasms that rebirthed
About the time you fell in love in Mexico
You climb on a volcano and are so grateful it isn't active and

doesn't erupt
You take your children around the world
You teach them about their ancestors
You teach them about love
You hold them until your arms can't hold themselves up
And on the day your time is up, your husband calls you darling
like he always does and tells you it's okay to let go, he watered
the plants already
And so, it is
And so, it is

FRONT YARD GETAWAY

Sometimes I cry more in a year than it rains.
Some days my loneliness doesn't feel as free.

Some nights I lay in bed and think, "Damn,
this is it? This is my life?" I get up early,

make coffee for myself. I play music
in the background. All the love songs

that end in tragedy. You know, the good ones.
I'm careful not to wake the children up too early

with my early morning passion. I tip-toe around
the wooden floors that creek decade-old secrets.

I sit in my front yard, attempt to make
a beachfront out of it. I let the sun use me.

She penetrates my skin like a lover. I stretch,
breathe, drink the greens I blended the day before.

I do all the things they tell you to do to manifest.
And then I wait. And I wait. And I wait.

For it to meet me halfway.
For life, to meet me halfway.

IT STILL BURNS WHEN YOU TOUCH IT

Most nights, we didn't hear the delicate begging between our legs. Our bruised cores sore for more than honey, for more than birthing 18-month-apart babies. We searched for impossible dreams that didn't ask us to abandon ourselves.

At 27, we took our voluptuous lands back. Snuck in through the alleyway of our stolen years. Lit the seams of our poorly sewn c-section scars on fire. Took back what belonged to us, burned it new, and renamed it something unholier.

Some nights I can still hear you in the whisper of the night telling me to repent the holes you placed on me on purpose. I still feel the holy water evaporate on my face when the priest tried to forgive me for asking, "Why would God hollow me if it's a sin to fill myself up?"

When he touched me between my legs, I didn't see God like they said I would. I didn't feel like the woman they said I'd be if I let him fuck me too soon, birth his child too soon, love him too soon. I knew after that my saving didn't need baptism or a boy. It only needed me.

Did the man they said I'll have to submit to forget I'm still breathing? I can't seem to find him when I go yelling his name. Where is he now that I've grown into these shoes? Into this woman? Into this burn?

MY DAUGHTER SARAH
written by my father Jaime Oropeza Sr. 6/16/ 2006

My eyes have seen no greater miracle
So much beauty, so much pain
So much love, so much hate
Have you found yourself yet
Do you look

Or are you waiting
The world is yours to have
All you need to do is want
Give it a chance
Let yourself go

Smile and they will smile
Love and they will love
Hate and they will hate
Live and they will live

Remember that you are a queen
A flower that is yet to bloom
A warm wind on a cold plain
A light where there is darkness

You have a chance at everything
Possibilities are endless
My eyes have seen no greater miracle
My daughter Sarah

ACKNOWLEDGEMENTS

I am beyond grateful for the love and support of my friends and family, who helped make this book possible. A huge thank you to my dear friends who helped with the editing. To my children, nephew, brothers, and sisters, this book is for us. The pain ends here. Mom and Dad, thank you for the gift of life, your sacrifices that still save me, and your undying love. Dad, thank you for the letters and poems you wrote when I was a child. You are the reason I write. And to my readers, thank you from the bottom of my heart. I am so grateful for your love.

Photo taken by Cris McCoy

Sarah Oropeza is a second-generation Mexican American poet
and artist from Kansas City, Kansas. She is a mother of two
children, and she graduated from the University of Kansas with a
bachelor's degree in psychology and a minor in sociology.
You can keep up with Sarah via social media:
@Ohsarahlee_
info@ohsarahlee.com

www.ingramcontent.com/pod-product-compliance
Lightning Source LLC
Chambersburg PA
CBHW050856150626
46549CB00013B/2515